T0162124

Contents

Part I

DOWN WITH THE ROYALS

Part I

Baby talk

Baby talk

ON A BALMY summer evening in late July 2013, I arrived at Buckingham Palace to find a curious spectacle. On one side of the Mall, within view of the palace, dozens if not hundreds of media organisations had set up their stalls, like a market selling second-hand broadcasting equipment. Thick cables snaked across the ground, catching the feet of the unwary, while excitable correspondents and bored camera crews waited for something to happen. Every now and then a reporter from somewhere in the world would start a piece-to-camera, pointing towards the palace gates and doing his or her best to disguise the fact that nothing had happened since the last bulletin. Deadlines passed, driving editors and producers mad

with frustration, but the gates remained stubbornly una-
dorned by the breathlessly anticipated (by the media, at
least) announcement of a royal birth. I had been invited
to take part in a live broadcast and at around 7.30 p.m.,
the news anchor standing next to me began a report for
her channel's main news programme of the day. Crowds
had gathered, she said, gesturing towards the palace, to
witness the moment when a royal servant would fix the
announcement to the railings. I could not resist cor-
recting her: crowds had *not* gathered, I pointed out. It
was actually a quiet evening for the height of the tourist
season, and the visitors who had turned out were easily
outnumbered by members of the press. (In the event,
it turned out that the Duchess of Cambridge's son had
already been born, but the announcement was held back
while the new parents got used to the arrival.)

Contrast this anecdote with a vignette from just over
a year earlier, when members of the royal family joined
a flotilla of small boats on the river Thames to mark
Elizabeth II's diamond jubilee. I did not think this was
something to celebrate, given that the same unelected
woman had been head of state since before I was born,

allowing me – and the rest of the population – no say in the matter. So I decided to join other republicans at a site on the south bank just outside City Hall, next to Tower Bridge, and take part in a demonstration calling for the replacement of the monarchy with a democratic system.

The protest was organised by Republic, the small but growing organisation that campaigns for an elected head of state. Its staff had negotiated in advance with the police and private security staff from local companies to ensure access to the riverbank on the day. The nearest Underground station was London Bridge and I arrived in the early afternoon to find the weather chilly and overcast, with occasional drizzle. At first I thought there were so many people in Tooley Street, which runs between London and Tower Bridges, because they were looking for shelter or somewhere to eat. Then, as I got closer to the Tower Bridge end of the street, I saw dozens of republican placards. I also spotted lines of private security guards blocking access to the protest site, and they flatly refused to let me through, even when I explained I was due to address the rally. In the end, I used my mobile to call one of the organisers and explain the problem; he told me that the numbers on the riverbank were being strictly controlled, regardless of the agreement Republic had made in advance of the demonstration, and he would have to ask one of the protesters to leave so I could join it. When I finally managed to reach the protest, I saw he was right; it had been limited to a narrow stretch of the riverbank, giving the impression from the river that few demonstrators had turned up. Later, when I'd made my speech, I returned to Tooley Street, where I climbed on a wall and addressed the much larger crowd of republicans who had not been allowed through.

So how did the press report this demonstration and the fact that hundreds of demonstrators had not been allowed through to the river? Here is *The Guardian*'s fair and accurate account, which included an acknowledgement that the small crowd of demonstrators on the riverbank were not the only republicans who had turned up:

> Amid the fanfare, it might seem like a difficult day for British republicans, but organisers of what was billed as the largest anti-monarchy protest of modern times say more than 1,000 people have joined them today.

Protesters from across the country began arriving at noon and have continued to stream into the two protest sites, according to the campaign group Republic.

Those taking part held anti-monarchy placards and chanted 'Monarchy out' while speakers including Joan Smith and Peter Tatchell have been addressing *the crowd* [my italics] throughout the afternoon.[1]

There was a crowd, but you wouldn't have known it if you happened to read the popular press. The biggest-selling newspapers didn't even make a stab at objective reporting, as this headline in the *Daily Mail* attests: 'Spoilsports! Anti-monarchists stage Thames riverside protest against Jubilee pageant but spectators drown them out with jeers'. The paper had its own bit of jeering to do, continuing in this vein:

The demonstrators gathered at Tower Bridge in a stunt organised by the campaign group Republic.

It bragged that hundreds of supporters from across

---

1   *The Guardian*, rolling news blog, 3 June 2012.

the country would descend on the capital for the 'biggest and boldest anti-monarchy protest of modern times'. In the end barely sixty showed up.[2]

This is simply untrue. The *Daily Mail* also claimed that the demonstrators 'taunted hundreds of families nearby', which certainly did not happen in the couple of hours I spent on the riverbank. The *Daily Express* took a similar line, with one of its columnists unable to resist gloating about the supposed turn-out:

> By far the biggest losers from the Jubilee have been the tiny, miserable band of republicans who have proved themselves snobbish elitists totally out of touch with public opinion.
>
> Chief executive of the anti-monarchist movement Graham Smith said that they planned to mount a protest at the river pageant which 'will give the Royal Family a rare glimpse of the strength of republican sentiment in Britain'.

2   Mail Online, 3 June 2012.

He was right about that. The size of the Republic group by the Thames on Sunday was minuscule, their whingeing voices drowned out by the pageant's foghorns and the public's enthusiastic renditions of the National Anthem.[3]

Even the picture captions were tendentious. In the *Daily Mail*, a picture of a cheerful protester holding up a rather mild-mannered message – 'I want a head of state to embody my values' – was captioned with the word 'Anger'. Thus, even polite displays of support for a democratic system are misreported, lest anyone get the idea that opposition to the monarchy is rational, principled and becoming more widespread.

The bias revealed in these anecdotes is habitual across the UK media, and is so ingrained that the people responsible barely seem aware of it. It goes hand in hand with the air of unreality that surrounds any event involving members of the British royal family, which would not be tolerated in any other walk of life. The

---

3   Leo McKinstry, *Daily Express*, 6 June 2012.

worst offenders are people described in all seriousness as 'royal correspondents', suggesting that they do a job analogous to other journalists. But this would be true only if defence correspondents went misty-eyed over men in uniform – 'the admiral was wearing a lovely uniform with a matching cap' – and asked inane questions about how much they liked their ships. In reality, journalistic rigour and indeed common sense go out of the window when it comes to royal 'stories', which often amount to no more than a member of the royal family wearing clothes, getting out of a car and walking along a street. Here is a typical royal story from the *Daily Mail* website: 'Blooming in black: Kate covers up her growing bump with £595 LBD as Duchess puts her severe morning sickness behind her in third public appearance since recovering from illness'. Like Princess Diana before her, the former Kate Middleton only has to wear the same coat twice to make headline news, with such mindless drivel regularly given the same prominence as famine in Africa or atrocities committed by Islamic State in Syria or Iraq.

In some degree, this is the legacy to the royals of the

late Princess Diana. She turned the family from a distant institution, which few people knew much about, into a branch of celebrity culture. Pitching for public sympathy in her battle with her estranged husband, Diana invited the media into her and their private lives, creating a form of royal soap opera. Many of her relatives-by-marriage didn't like it, especially when the Princess's sudden death in 1997 sent her popularity soaring and stuffier members of the family (including the Queen) found themselves called on to emote in public. Total strangers had no such inhibitions; on the morning after the fatal car crash in Paris, I was on my way to a BBC studio in Portland Place in central London when I spotted a homemade poster fixed to a lamp-post. It was well above head height, although I suppose that bringing a ladder was no trouble to someone who had gone to the effort of finding a photo of the Princess *and* a 'picture' of Jesus; he or she had pasted them on a large piece of card with a caption reading, 'If Jesus was the Son of God, who is Diana?' Nor was that the limit of the madness: on the evening before the Princess's funeral, I was startled to hear a Radio 4 presenter introduce an interview with a man who had had an 18-inch portrait of Diana tattooed on his thigh. Even the late Princess, with her insatiable appetite for the attention of total strangers, might have baulked at this 'tribute'. Such anecdotes illustrate two iron rules of royal 'stories': nothing much happens most of the time, and reporters end up trying to extract sound bites from people they'd normally run a mile to avoid.

One effect of Diana's unexpected death was that the monarchy got its most recent crisis in early, before bankers and MPs, and has had longer to recover. In that sense, the Princess did the royals a favour in the long run, stimulating an appetite for royal 'news' that fireproofed the family against temporary spurts of unpopularity. Much of what passes for royal 'reporting' is trivial, fawning and uncritical; actions that the rest of us carry out every day, without too much expense of effort, are greeted as something remarkable. The standard riposte of editors, on the rare occasions that they are challenged about this saturation coverage of the royal family, is that they are merely responding to public demand. They point to the crowds who turn out for royal events, ignoring the huge numbers of people who aren't interested and don't bother to turn up. In the run-up to the wedding of Kate Middleton and Prince William in 2011, we were told that an excited populace couldn't wait for the event and that street parties were being organised up and down the country. Then a story appeared in the *Daily Telegraph* revealing that so many people were *leaving* the country that the charity that organises street parties was urging people to postpone them. It went on:

> The move comes as travel agents report a 'massive' surge in inquiries about holidays around April 29, when Prince William and Kate Middleton are to marry at Westminster Abbey.
>
> There had been expectations that the event would lead to a mass influx of visitors, boosting the economy.
>
> But with four months to go, even online travel sites, usually dominated by last-minute bookings, have reported an increase in bookings around the wedding period.[4]

---

4 *Daily Telegraph*, 1 January 2011.

Something similar happened the following year, at the time of another costly obsession, the diamond jubilee. Before it happened, the Centre for Retail Research predicted that the event would 'boost UK spending by almost £509 million'; it claimed that a small drop in output caused by the double bank holiday would be more than offset by increases in spending on souvenirs and tourism, predicting a net boost to the economy of £409 million.[5] But the governor of the Bank of England, Mervyn King, sounded a warning note when he appeared before a House of Lords committee, suggesting that the jubilee could throw the economy into reverse; he said it was 'quite possible' that UK output would contract in the second quarter of 2012 as a result of the extra holiday.[6] Opinion polls suggested he was right to dampen expectations, with only a third of people saying they would personally be celebrating the jubilee; fully half the population said they didn't intend to celebrate

---

5   Centre of Retail Research: Queen's Diamond Jubilee: Retail impact of £508.94 million.

6   *The Guardian*, 27 March 2012.

it at all. Fifty-two per cent said they would watch it at home on TV, which didn't bode well for predictions of lavish public spending.[7] King was proved right later in the year when the Office for National Statistics estimated that the event had shaved between 0.3 and 0.4 per cent off GDP. The *FT* reported:

> The effect of the two extra days off in June to mark the Queen's coronation in 1952 was largely felt by companies in the UK's dominant services sector, which accounts for more than three-quarters of GDP.
>
> The ONS noted that output in the sector dropped by 1.4 per cent between May and June. The falls were widespread across all service industries, with the exception of government.[8]

In a decade when the family seemed intent on producing annual extravaganzas even though the country was in the grip of a punishing economic recession, the next

---

7 Recent YouGov Polling on the Monarchy and the Jubilee – Media Briefing.

8 *Financial Times*, 17 May 2013.

big royal event was the birth of Prince George. More or less from the day she got engaged, Kate Middleton had rarely appeared in public without a supporting cast of bashful children or teenagers; in a dynasty where gender roles are fixed in stone (if not the Stone Age), it may be that this amounted to a series of prompts, reminding her that her duty lay in pregnancy and motherhood. She duly obliged on that July day in 2013, giving birth in the private wing of St Mary's hospital in Paddington, a mile or so north of Buckingham Palace. No one knew anything about the infant, other than the fact that he was a healthy boy, but he nevertheless displaced his Uncle Harry as third in line to the throne. The whole notion of the royal succession is innately ridiculous, but Harry's displacement made it visibly so; the notion that a tiny baby automatically has the qualities to do anything, whether it's becoming a plumber or a monarch, belongs in the Middle Ages.

Nevertheless, hordes of reporters had been camped for days outside the private wing of St Mary's hospital, to the considerable inconvenience of sick people and their relatives, who found parking spaces suspended.

Most of the time there was nothing to report, forcing correspondents to fall back on the desperate standby of interviewing former royal 'aides' or each other. One of the most choice moments for me was hearing the Queen's former press secretary, interviewed outside Buckingham Palace, talk about the 'people's pregnancy'. I don't know if he really intended to implicate the entire male population over the age of puberty in the conception, but an even more imaginative species of paternity was implied by a man who joined the media scrum outside the hospital. Asked by a reporter about a rolled-up canvas he had brought with him to the vigil, he eagerly unrolled it to reveal a painting that appeared to show the Duchess of Cambridge as the Virgin Mary. The normal human response to this species of derangement is an instinctive recoil, but that's a problem on live television; when the man launched into an explanation about the Duchess's first child being the reincarnation of Jesus Christ, the flustered reporter cut him off in mid-flow.

There have been occasions, in recent years, when I almost convinced myself that sycophancy towards the royal family must have reached its nadir. I'm always wrong, and the birth of Prince George revealed new levels of inanity across the print and broadcast media. Even *The Guardian* produced what it called 'live royal baby coverage', giving the infant's weight and quoting this earth-shattering remark from Prince William: 'We could not be happier.'[9] On the day after the birth, when the couple were expected to appear outside the hospital for the infant's first picture opportunity, some networks actually transmitted 'live' footage of a stubbornly unopened door. I don't know how the door felt but the belated appearance of the Duke and Duchess prompted a frenzy of excitement among the assembled journalists, who shouted banal questions without evident embarrassment. In the press, Middleton's appearance precipitated a minute exegesis of her hair, her dress and her swollen stomach – hardly unexpected in a woman who had so recently given birth. It was a small price to pay for the priceless positive spin generated by the event, explaining why royal aides sometimes claim that they don't *need* to manipulate the media. The

---

9   *The Guardian*, rolling news blog, 23 July 2013.

claim may be disingenuous – I'm sure a huge amount of planning goes into every royal 'event' – but it is true that they are working in an unusually receptive environment.

But they bring tourists here

One of the 'justifications' most frequently offered for keeping the royal family is that their milestones boost tourism to the UK. The assumption that royal events, and the mere existence of the family, bring foreign visitors pouring into the country is made so automatically that hardly anyone thinks to question it. In a period when royal celebrations have come thick and fast – Prince William's wedding, the diamond jubilee, the birth of Prince George – it should not be hard to test this proposition. The results are revealing: there is actually no evidence to suggest that the British royal family makes the UK a uniquely popular holiday destination. On the contrary, any such notion is dispelled by the simple expedient at looking at tourist numbers and revenue worldwide.

But first I want to go back in time and look at the

effect on visitor numbers of two specific events, namely the weddings of the Queen's elder sons, Prince Charles in 1981 and Prince Andrew in 1986. The first of these drew worldwide attention, so much so that still photographs from the day, such as Charles and Diana kissing before crowds on a balcony at Buckingham Palace, remain instantly recognisable. This type of public ceremony is often described as something the UK does better than any other country, making us the envy of other nations, so surely it drew tourists in their hundreds of thousands? The answer, when Republic made a request under the Freedom of Information (FOI) Act to the publicly funded national tourism agency, Visit-Britain, was instructive. According to the organisation's head of research and forecasting:

> If we look at the marriage of Andrew and Sarah in July 1986, we find that across the year as a whole there were 4 per cent fewer visitors to Britain than in 1985, but that in July there were 8 per cent fewer than in July of 1985. While this and the results relating to 1981 are inconclusive, such as it is, the evidence points to royal

weddings having *a negative impact on inbound tour-ism* [my italics].[10]

The idea that foreigners who are planning holidays abroad sit down with a list of republics versus nations with hereditary heads of state has always struck me as implausible. If this proposition were true, you would expect to find the UK, Belgium, the Nether-lands, Norway, Sweden and Spain dominating the top ten destinations in the world, drawn up by the UN World Travel Organization.[11] So which country has the highest number of international tourist arrivals? The answer is France, which has been a republic since Napo-leon III went into exile (in England, of course) after being defeated in the Franco-Prussian War of 1870–71. France easily beat every other country in the world in terms of foreign tourists in 2012, clocking up 83 million tourist arrivals; many more people visited France than actually live there (66 million). The US, which is also

10 *The Guardian*, 19 July 2013.

11 UNTWO Tourism Highlights, 2014 edition, p. 6.

a republic, was in second place with 66.7 million. And where was the UK in all this? At number eight, with only 29.3 million visitors. There was a monarchy, Spain, in the top five, but that almost certainly had more to do with beaches, landscape and stunning tourist attractions than the country's deeply unpopular royal family. The *Daily Mail* reported these figures with an unintentionally revealing headline: 'France *crowned* [my italics] most popular country in the world with record-breaking number of tourists (and UK lags in eighth place, beaten by Spain, Italy and even Germany)'.[12]

Even if we look at the economic impact of tourism, rather than the number of international tourist arrivals, there is no evidence that monarchy is a big draw. The US has the highest tourist receipts by far, amounting to $139.6 billion in 2013; in this top ten, Spain moves up a place to number two with $60.4 billion, but France ($56.1 billion) is close behind. The UK, sadly, drops a place in this table, coming in at number nine ($40.6 billion).

As France has discovered, one of the advantages of

---

12 Mail Online, 13 August 2014.

becoming a republic is that the sumptuous palaces and huge land holdings which used to belong to the royal family can be thrown open to the public; the Palace of Versailles is the third biggest tourist attraction in the country, after the Louvre and the Eiffel Tower, with around five million visitors a year. According to the Labour MP Margaret Hodge, who chairs the House of Commons public accounts committee, Buckingham Palace is 'only open seventy-eight days a year' and 'they only have about half a million visitors'.[13] There is an option for an 'exclusive guided tour' of the state rooms during the winter months, but the cost – £75 per person, including a glass of champagne and a discount on purchases in the shop – is prohibitive for anyone who is on a low income.[14] It isn't even as though the royal family does a good job of looking after the many grand houses and palaces currently in its stewardship, as the public accounts committee discovered. I shall return to this point later, but let's go back for a moment to the birth of Prince George, and the wildly

---

13 BBC News Politics, 28 January 2014.

14 Royal Collection Trust website.

over-optimistic predictions made about the impact of his arrival at home and abroad.

The idea of a universally joyful populace, splashing money on souvenirs and dutifully waving Union Jacks, was uncritically reported by most of the UK media. Yet there was evidence, if anyone had bothered to look, that this notion was nowhere near the truth. A You-Gov report[15] based on polling in July 2013 suggested that slightly more British adults (53 per cent) were uninterested in the birth, compared to 46 per cent who did take an interest. Almost a quarter of the population (24 per cent) was 'not at all interested', while another 29 per cent was 'not very interested'. In the circumstances, any headline (and there were many) attributing positive feelings to 'everyone' or 'the country' was bound to be wrong. That didn't stop the national tourist board, VisitEngland, publishing a breathless press release which claimed that 'England is all in a frenzy over the arrival of the Duke and Duchess of Cambridge's baby son'.[16]

---

15 'Who's interested in the Royal baby?' YouGov, 23 July 2013.

16 VisitEngland Statement: Impact of Royal Baby on Tourism.

According to the organisation's chairman [*sic*], Lady Cobham, 'the Royal Family has long been an asset to English tourism, but never more so than right now, with people across the world in a fever pitch of excitement around the arrival of the royal baby'. The press release babbled about 'global excitement', apparently unaware of how tasteless and Anglocentric this view was against the background of a savage civil war in Syria and a refugee crisis of massive proportions in neighbouring countries. Were any of these tragic fugitives really inclined to go on VisitEngland's website and click on a link to 'royal baby-inspired breaks and packages'? Did they hanker after the Hilton hotel's 'Tot-ter around Kensington' package where 'guests can enjoy a two-night shopping break, ideal for mother-and-daughter bonding and mums-to-be'? Baby talk is an apt name for much of the nonsense spoken and written in the UK about the royal family, as another offer highlighted by VisitEngland suggested: 'Meanwhile, one of the luxury suites at the Grosvenor House hotel on Park Lane has been transformed into a five-star nursery for jet-setting babies. The hotel has ... transformed a Premium

Park View Suite into a quintessential English nursery, designed and tailored with a royal baby in mind.'

In November 2014, Lady Cobham was awarded a CBE for services to tourism by the Prince of Wales, an occasion only slightly marred by an altercation between her partner, the former Conservative Cabinet minister David Mellor, and a London taxi driver.

Not long after the royal birth, the *Evening Standard* declared Kate Middleton's child, by then aged all of two months, the 'most influential person in London' – quite a feat for someone who had yet to speak his first word. The paper gushed:

> The eight-week-old son of the Duke and Duchess of Cambridge was chosen because he has become the capital's biggest global ambassador.
>
> The baby Prince eclipsed Mayor Boris Johnson, who topped the list of London's most influential people a year ago.[17]

---

17 *Evening Standard*, 20 September 2013.

Inevitably, one of the reasons for this thoroughly unde-
served accolade was the infant's supposed impact on
– you guessed it – tourism. The paper's editor, Sarah
Sands, who had previously been one of the Mayor's
biggest supporters, trilled:

> London is a magnet for the rest of the world and our new-
> est power resident, Prince George, is a timely symbol.
> He is our greatest tourist attraction, along with his
> great-grandmother, which is why he has been chosen
> this year as the first among Londoners.

How is a baby supposed to function as a tourist attraction? Are foreign visitors drawn to London merely in the
hope of breathing the same air as this unusually gifted
infant? Or are they supposed to think that London is a
small, informal city where a royal baby might be encoun-
tered in shops or public spaces? If so, they might be in
for a shock: the Duke and Duchess of Cambridge are
no more keen than any other parent to find their infant
son the focus of unsolicited attention from strangers.
In 2014, lawyers for the couple warned a photographer

called Niraj Tanna to 'cease harassing' Prince George and his nanny after he was spotted by royal protection officers in Battersea Park. A statement from Kensington Palace accused Tanna of 'placing Prince George under surveillance' and suggested his behaviour amounted to stalking.[18] The photographer denied harassment and insisted that he was entitled to take pictures in a public park.

In fact, there has been a sea change in attitudes towards children's privacy in recent years, and photographing them without their parents' consent is regarded as beyond the pale by most editors. When adults die in tragic circumstances, family photographs are often published with children's faces obscured, a practice which was unknown in newspapers three decades ago. There is also much greater sensitivity than there used to be about the need to avoid sexualising babies and young children. None of this seems to have registered with the editorial team at *Vanity Fair* magazine when they decided to produce an issue marking the first birthday of Prince George in 2014. The cover

---

18   BBC News, 2 October 2014.

was given over to an informal photograph of William and Kate, the latter grinning and holding their son. The strapline read: 'Happy Birthday, Prince George! Raising the World's Most Eligible Infant'.[19]

Eligible for *what*? Inside, the magazine devoted nine-and-a-half pages to drivel about the Prince's christening, revealing the make of pram chosen by the couple – 'navy blue, top-of-the-line Silver Cross' – and describing the baby blue monogrammed sweater given to him as a Christmas gift by his grandfather, the Prince of Wales. The magazine went on to claim that the baby had 'united the royals with commoners', a choice of language which was telling in itself. It suggested that the magazine is living in a fantasy version of the UK where cheerful working-class people doff their caps to the royals as they pass and food banks are unknown.

Succession blues

It was left to the YouGov poll I've already mentioned to

---

19 *Vanity Fair*, August 2014.

pour a welcome bucket of cold water on such extrava-
gant claims, while a breakdown of the results contained a
warning for the future of the monarchy. The poll showed
that Conservative voters were much more likely to be
interested in the birth than Labour supporters, which is
unsurprising; many left-of-centre politicians are instinctive republicans, even if they are reluctant to admit it
publicly. But the gender difference was striking: many
more women than men were following the event, and
female commentators showed a marked preference for
a female baby. If the scenes following Diana's death
had revealed a previously unremarked tendency among
women to identify with female members of the royal
family, it became apparent that a generation of women
who had grown up in the meantime was now hoping
for a new Princess. They were to be disappointed, and
that is why the birth of a male third in line to the throne
was and is bad news for the monarchy. The UK had a
female head of state for almost half of the twentieth century and the Queen is still carrying out royal 'duties'
– if looking tired and grumpy on occasion – in the first
decade-and-a-half of the twenty-first. But the arrival of

Prince George means that all the monarchy has to offer
for the remainder of the century is an unbroken line of
three kings: the Queen's pantomimic eldest son, *his* eldest son and *his* eldest son. Even if they adopt different
names on succeeding to the throne, as the Queen's uncle
David (Edward VIII) did, it is now written in stone that
the UK's next three heads of state will be Charles, William and George Windsor. Barring accidents, at least two
of them are unlikely to ascend the throne before their six-
ties or seventies; age on its own is not a reason for ruling
someone out of a job, but a royal family with genes for
longevity, and access to state-of-the-art health care, is a
recipe for what is effectively a gerontocracy. That is one
of the reasons why younger members of the family have
had to be deployed so extensively on ceremonial occasions, not just to lift some of the burden from the Queen
but to obscure the fact that the country's ceremonial head
is approaching ninety. As I write, and assuming that Elizabeth Windsor remains in good health, that birthday is
only a year away. No doubt the public celebrations are
already being planned and cost will not be a considera-
tion, however weak the state of the economy.

The royal family depends for its existence on such milestones, which provide a series of public spectacles designed to suggest that the institution is essentially ceremonial and harmless. This is a fantasy, concealing the extensive influence of the royal family on public life, but it means that the then Archbishop of Canterbury spoke with greater accuracy than he knew when he described the marriage of the Prince of Wales and Lady Diana Spencer as 'the stuff of which fairy tales are made'. Actually, it would be more accurate to say that fairy stories and gossip are what we get in relation to the royals: even during the family's *anni horribiles* in the late 1990s, we heard a great deal more about schisms within the extended family – Diana versus Charles, Diana versus Camilla Parker Bowles, Charles versus Earl Spencer – than any serious interrogation of the institution. In that sense, 'modernisation' of the royal family consisted not of a conversation about democracy, representation and accountability, but of soap opera-style reporting of conflicts between individuals.

Something similar had happened before, when George IV excluded his estranged wife, Caroline of Brunswick, from his coronation in 1821; Caroline was refused entry to Westminster Abbey and fell ill that same evening, dying less than three weeks later amid rumours that she had been poisoned. Caroline's popularity with the masses is a reminder that factionalism has always existed in the family and is survivable, perhaps even more so in an age of mass media, when the public's emotions are so easy to manipulate. The failure of Diana's marriage, her death and her ex-husband's relationship with Camilla Parker Bowles provided reams of material for celebrity culture, humanising figures who would otherwise have appeared cold and distant; predictions that the public would 'never accept' Camilla always seemed wide of the mark, not least because there was nothing much they could do about it. And while becoming fodder for gossip magazines may not have been entirely comfortable for older members of the family, the willingness of the next generation to cooperate with the kind of journalism pioneered by *Hello!* magazine demonstrates how easily they have adapted to it. The benefits are enormous: the phrase used by so many people after Diana's death – 'She was just like us' – is telling, for of course members of the royal family are categorically *not* like us. Diana had an unhappy marriage but she was one of the most privileged single mothers in the country, able to command the attention of politicians, prelates, editors and foreign dignitaries.

One of the reasons the monarchy has survived, in other words, is the near-complete suspension of normal journalistic scrutiny, either in terms of the cost of the institution or the archaic assumptions on which it rests. Thus Prince Charles is mocked – somewhat affectionately, it has to be said – for his unfamiliarity with the functions of everyday life, but the contradiction of having an unelected head of state in a 21st-century democracy goes almost unquestioned. This should be borne in mind when monarchists cite opinion polls showing overwhelming support for the royal family, sometimes reaching a figure as high as 80 per cent in recent years. No mainstream political party has *ever* called for a debate on the monarchy, let alone come out against it, leaving a vacuum at the heart of public life. At the same time, opinion poll questions are often posed in a way that favours the status quo; it is a well-known fact that responses are influenced by how a question is asked, and respondents are rarely offered a viable-sounding alternative. There is a world of difference between asking 'Do you support the Queen?' and asking 'Would you like to vote for the person who represents the country?' Nor is it safe to assume that the popularity of the monarchy is written in stone: huge social changes often come about, in retrospect, in a relatively short period of time. Take just one example of how British attitudes have altered radically, and for the better, in my lifetime: I was born in a period when homosexuality was punishable by law; since then, I have watched it go through a process of decriminalisation, growing public acceptance, legal recognition of civil partnerships and finally gay marriage. Who but the most committed campaigner for social justice would have envisaged all that in 1957, when it was first suggested that gay people should not face criminal sanctions?

The British monarchy is an aberration in the modern world, a point I shall return to in a later section, but for the moment it is worth noting that there is far from universal confidence that it will survive. An Ipsos MORI poll in 2012 suggested that three out of five Britons are confident it will last half a century, but the figure falls to 42 per cent when people are asked about one hundred years' time.[20] We also know that in nation after nation, once the supposedly unthinkable happens, public opinion adapts to the new situation. Elected presidents have proved popular in many countries, including Ireland, where two of the people who have held the office – the human rights campaigner Mary Robinson, and the poet and former culture minister Michael Higgins – are widely admired; in South Africa, Nelson Mandela achieved a species of secular sainthood, while Liberia's Ellen Johnson Sirleaf has been one of the leading voices urging the world to take action against the Ebola outbreak.

Whatever happened to free speech?

This makes it even odder that arguments for a different constitutional arrangement have barely been aired

---

20 Jubilee Debate: The Queen & The Monarchy, Latest findings on British public opinion, Ipsos MORI, 19 November 2012.

in the UK. Republican voices are mocked or silenced in a way that would be regarded as an assault on free speech in more enlightened countries, even on the supposedly neutral BBC. I've lost count of the number of times I've heard 'debates' about the monarchy which exclude voices questioning its existence; one of the most recent was a discussion on Radio 4's *Today* programme about whether Muslim as well as Christian texts should be included at the next coronation, with no one asking the obvious question of why we should have such an event in the twenty-first century. Even seasoned broadcasters struggle to achieve 'balance', as I found when I was invited to appear on another Radio 4 programme, the *Moral Maze*, in the run-up to the diamond jubilee. I had barely been introduced by the presenter, Michael Buerk, when the former Conservative Defence Secretary Michael Portillo launched into a barrage of sneers; his opening sally was that my opposition to the monarchy must be motivated by envy of the Queen. Portillo interrupted me time after time, to the growing agitation of Michael Buerk, who finally grabbed him by the arm in an attempt to shut him up. The programme prompted dozens of complaints from listeners as Roger Bolton, the presenter of Radio 4's *Feedback* programme, acknowledged in a blog:

> Michael [Buerk] seems to paddle calmly over the surface of the water, seamlessly directing affairs.
>
> However this week on *Feedback* we had a number of emails suggesting that he hadn't done his job in last week's edition about the monarchy, and allowed one of the witnesses, a particularly feisty Joan Smith, to be 'trampled' by Michael Portillo.[21]

It's that word again: 'feisty' is always used about women who stand up for themselves, and rarely, if ever, about men. But an accurate critique of Portillo's behaviour wouldn't focus on his manners, appalling though they were. Republicans are entitled to free speech, just like anyone else, and I had been invited onto the programme to explain my reasons for opposing the monarchy as an institution. Portillo's reaction to my presence in the

---

21 Radio 4 and 4 Extra Blog, Feedback: The Moral Maze, 17 February 2012.

studio felt like an attempt, conscious or otherwise, to exclude the argument for an elected head of state from the mainstream media.

Even something as reasonable as putting the current royals in a historical context is liable to be grotesquely misrepresented. In February 2013, the novelist Hilary Mantel gave a lecture at the British Museum, published a couple of weeks later in the *London Review of Books*,[22] about the anachronistic status of the royal family in modern life. Mantel, who had previously achieved near 'national treasure' status for her Booker prize-winning novels set in the reign of Henry VIII, looked at the royals almost as zoological specimens, comparing them at one point to pandas ('pandas and royal persons alike are expensive to conserve and ill-adapted to any modern environment'). She compared Princess Diana to Marie Antoinette, and suggested that Kate Middleton 'appeared to have been designed and built by craftsmen'.

The lecture was clearly a reflection on the unchanging nature of royalty, not a personal attack, so Mantel must

---

22 *London Review of Books*, Vol. 35, No. 4, 21 February 2013.

have been astonished to find herself pilloried in the *Daily Mail*.[23] Under the headline 'Bring Up The Bodies author Hilary Mantel's venomous attack on Kate Middleton', the paper pulled no punches: 'A best-selling author who has based her literary career on writing about the Royal Family has launched a bitter attack on the Duchess of Cambridge. Hilary Mantel used her position among the novel-writing elite to make an astonishing and venomous critique of Kate.'

Other papers quickly piled in. *The Sun* described Mantel as a 'snooty writer' and said she had 'insultingly dismissed' the Duchess;[24] the *Daily Express* detected a 'backlash' against Mantel as 'a host of politicians and celebrities … rallied to defend the honour of the future Queen'.[25] There was such a storm that the Prime Minister decided to get involved, despite the fact that he was on an official visit to India and might be assumed to have more important things to talk about; Cameron

---

23 *Daily Mail*, 19 February 2013.

24 *The Sun*, 20 February 2013.

25 *Daily Express*, 20 February 2013.

condemned Mantel's observations about the Duchess as 'completely misguided and completely wrong'. Even the leader of the Labour Party, Ed Miliband, felt he had to say something, describing Mantel's remarks as 'pretty offensive' and saying that 'Kate Middleton is doing a brilliant job in a difficult role'.[26]

A few months later, my book *The Public Woman* was published. One of the chapters, which picked up themes I had written about in my earlier book *Misogynies*, used Middleton as an exemplar of the remarkably limited role of women in the royal family. The rest of the book looked at the continuing failure across the world to grant women full human rights, ranging across subjects such as FGM and trafficking for labour and sexual exploitation. But it was my remarks about the Duchess that were picked up and misrepresented, just like Mantel's, as a personal attack. The *Daily Mail* returned to the fray, describing my observations as a 'blistering attack'.[27] The paper's columnist, Richard Kay, wrote:

---

26 *Daily Express*, 20 February 2013.

27 *Daily Mail*, 22 May 2013.

After the furore over Hilary Mantel's venomous attack on the Duchess of Cambridge, whom she described as a 'shop-window mannequin' with a 'plastic smile', you might have thought writers would think twice about putting pen to paper on the subject.

Not a bit of it.

For just three months after the Booker Prize-winner faced a furious backlash for her comments – which even earned a reprimand from the Prime Minister – human rights activist Joan Smith dismisses the former Kate Middleton as 'unambitious and bland' and Britain's 'Queen Wag'.[28]

Kay barely bothered to conceal his wish that critics of the royals would just keep quiet. But the refusal of the media to give a fair hearing to rational analysis of the royal family reached its *reductio ad absurdum* when an American showbiz blogger, Perez Hilton, came swinging into the ring. Why on earth would I express reservations about Middleton or Princess Diana? Hilton had

---

28   *Daily Mail*, 21 May 2013.

no doubts: 'Wow,' he exclaimed. 'Talk about harsh!!
It might be time to retract the claws, Joan!'[29] It was
an unintentionally pertinent observation, exposing the
journalistic impulse to turn each and every critique of
the UK royals into a cat fight.

In an atmosphere so inflamed on the subject of monarchy, any perceived 'insult' to a member of the family
runs the risk of prompting irrational and disproportion-
ate reactions. I thoroughly dislike the kind of childish
prank played by two Australian radio DJs, Mel Greig
and Michael Christian, during the Duchess of Cambridge's first pregnancy, but not because it involved one
of the royals; it would have been indefensible no matter
who the target was. In December 2012, Greig and Christian called the London hospital where the Duchess was
being treated for extreme morning sickness, pretending
to be the Queen and Prince Charles; I don't suppose
they expected to get very far, but an Indian-born nurse,
Jacintha Saldanha, was taken in. She put them through
to a colleague, who disclosed details of the Duchess's

---

29 Perezhilton.com, May 2013.

condition and treatment; it was a distasteful breach of privacy but no lasting harm was done to any member of the royal family. The radio station went ahead and broadcast the stunt in Australia, where listeners mocked the DJs' dreadful attempt at upper-class British accents, and it was subsequently reported around the world. The whole thing was a storm in a tea cup but the impact on Ms Saldanha was catastrophic. A couple of days later, she hanged herself.

To anyone who is not invested in the 'specialness' of the royal family, it is hard to comprehend that someone would take so much responsibility on themselves as a consequence of accidental involvement in a stupid hoax. In September 2014, a nurse at the same hospital told an inquest that Ms Saldanha felt responsible for the release of private information about the Duchess, while another colleague said she received an email in which Ms Saldanha talked about feeling 'ashamed'.[30] Even so the coroner, Dr Fiona Wilcox, did not criticise the DJs and made the important point that Ms Saldanha's death 'was

---

30 *Daily Mirror*, 12 September 2014.

not reasonably foreseeable'.[31] Yet, in the days immediately after her suicide, some users of social networking sites moved swiftly from shock to rage and began to make the absurd claim that the DJs had 'wanted' this outcome all along. Greig apologised to Ms Saldanha's family at the inquest but she also told the BBC's *Newsnight* programme about the death threats she received: 'I was in lockdown for months. There were bullets with our names on it sent to police stations.'[32] She said that the threats to herself and her family continued for eighteen months.

This is a tragic story but it raises a subject which is sensitive and rarely discussed. Ms Saldanha seems to have felt genuine affection towards the royal family, but that is not automatically the case among immigrants to the UK. Some people who were not born here feel there is an expectation that they should defer to its institutions, to the extent of internalising a kind of patriotism even more onerous than that which is placed on the

---

31 Digital Spy, 12 September 2014.

32 *The Independent*, 13 October 2014.

indigenous population. Even on the left, some people defend immigration by pointing out how much recent arrivals to this country 'love' the royal family. It is a form of stereotyping – a demand that they should display their adopted 'Britishness' – which makes many first- and second-generation immigrants uncomfortable. Some of them might reasonably argue, in an atmosphere of growing hostility to foreigners, that they don't feel able to say that they have no particular admiration for the royal family. If home-grown republicans regularly risk the wrath of the *Daily Mail*, a newspaper not known for its warm embrace of immigrants, how much harder is it for foreigners to criticise the monarchy?

At the very least, this tragic sequence of events is a reminder that we should be acutely aware of the danger of investing royal personages with exaggerated significance. There is a dark underside to a constant diet of royal trivia, encouraging people to regard the royals as not just different from the rest of us but creatures who need to be wrapped in cotton wool. Some individuals identify with members of the family to an extent that isn't healthy, as the reaction to Princess Diana's death showed in 1997. On that occasion, bunches of flowers and sentimental messages outside Kensington Palace co-existed uncomfortably with outbursts of anger towards those of us who were not in mourning and did not feel personally touched by the death of someone we had never met. This fluctuation between sentimentality and intolerance is among many reasons why we urgently need a calm, rational and grown-up discussion about the monarchy in this country. What would such an unthink-able conversation look like? That's the subject I'm going to address in the next section.

Part II

Down with the royals

I F WE FORGET about the Windsors as individuals for a moment, the most powerful arguments against a hereditary monarchy are that it is undemocratic, expensive and unaccountable. I am going to address the arguments in that order, and the first two are easily dealt with. The third element, the royal family's extensive political interference and influence, needs more space because it has been quite deliberately concealed from us. At a time when most public institutions and individuals, including MPs, have been held up to minute and often painful scrutiny, it is an extraordinary fact that since 2010 the monarchy has enjoyed complete immunity from requests under the FOI Act. Even when members of the family *are* told to hand over correspondence from an earlier period which shows the extent of their influence, ministers are on hand to veto publication, leading to lengthy (and publicly funded) court battles. But first I want to look at the nonsensical idea that a single family should own the privilege, in perpetuity, of providing heads of state for a country of more than 60 million people.

If we were told that the UK's prime ministers would in future be drawn from a single family – the descendants of John Major, say, or Tony Blair – there would rightly be an outcry. Even when family members of former PMs harbour political ambitions, as one of Blair's sons does, there is no automatic route into the House of Commons; they are expected to state their party allegiance, reveal their political views and stand for election to the House of Commons like anyone else. And while the prospect of the Prince of Wales going on the stump, addressing meetings in town halls and draughty community centres, is admittedly quite appealing, it is also improbable. What could he say? In 2013, Charles reached what used to be the standard male retirement age of sixty-five without ever having had a proper job. Most of his political interventions are shrouded in secrecy, as we shall see, and his credentials amount to little more than the single word he uttered at the diamond jubilee concert: 'Mummy'. As Charles knows very well, the whole point of hereditary monarchy is that it allows people like him to bypass the inconvenient chores associated with democracy, such as knocking on doors and trying to persuade sceptical voters. The consequence is a system that fails every single test of diversity and equality, a fact that has been dimly grasped by at least some of Europe's remaining monarchies. In several countries, elderly kings or queens have started worrying about their dwindling popularity and abdicated in favour of the next generation; so far it has happened in Belgium, the Netherlands and Spain. The latter's King Juan Carlos I – of whom we shall hear more later – is said to have observed that he didn't want his son, the Prince of Asturias, 'to grow old waiting for the throne like Prince Charles'.[33] But even such limited acknowledgements of the system's shortcomings are too radical for the UK,

---

33 *Daily Telegraph*, 8 June 2014.

where the Queen clings tenaciously to office after (as I write) almost sixty-three years on the throne. Once she dies, the *de facto* list of people excluded from becoming head of state for at least three generations will go like this: no women, no black people, no Asians, no Jews and certainly no Catholics (still barred by law). I also doubt whether we'll see an openly secular or gay king, unless the royal family changes dramatically.

As well as being unrepresentative, the system is unnecessarily expensive. The cost of providing for an entire family is obviously much greater than funding the office of an elected head of state, whose relatives would rarely, if ever, be required to undertake public duties. The royal finances are another area where most of the British media fail to do their job, producing annual good-news stories with headlines like this one: 'What a bargain! How the royal family costs you just 56p a year'.[34] That figure is arrived at by dividing the 'cost' of the monarchy, estimated at £35.7 million in 2013, by the population of the UK. This means of calculation is

---

34 *Daily Express*, 26 June 2014.

very useful to the monarchy, producing quotes like this one from the editor of a royal magazine: 'The monarchy is exceptionally good value at 56p per person. We are looking at money for the Royal Family performing all their official duties. I know some people won't agree but I think it still represents an excellent use of public money.'[35] Most of this is nonsense, as a closer look at the royal finances shows. Even if we were to accept the figure of almost £36 million at face value, the British monarchy is still one of the most expensive in Europe. A report published by Republic[36] suggests that Sweden's monarchy has an annual cost of £15 million, Denmark £13 million and Luxembourg £9 million. The Netherlands and Norway are above the official UK figure, at £40 million and £41 million respectively, but the problem with such comparisons is that the British total excludes huge costs to taxpayers. One significant element that doesn't appear in the official estimates is the

---

35 Joe Little, editor of *Majesty* magazine, quoted in the *Daily Express*, ibid.

36 'Worth Every Penny? The real cost of the monarchy to British taxpayers', published by Republic (www.republic.org.uk).

cost of providing security for numerous members of the British royal family, along with the bill for royal visits. The security figure is particularly contentious because it includes providing protection for the Queen's relatives when they are not performing official duties, which is almost certainly why we are banned from knowing it; at a time when public services are being cut to the bone, taxpayers might look askance if they knew how much of their money is spent on police escorts for shopping trips and visits to nightclubs. Republic estimates the cost of royal security at around £100 million; adding in other likely costs, such as £21.5 million for royal visits, Republic believes that the annual cost of the British monarchy is in the region of £300 million. Of course, we can't know this for certain, and I'm sure the royal household would question its accuracy, but the answer is simple: if the monarchy has nothing to fear, why doesn't it publish full accounts instead of leaving out the most expensive elements? No other public institution would get away with this sleight of hand, denying essential financial information from the public which bears the cost. But then it is not even as if the royal household manages the

Queen's finances efficiently; a report published by the House of Commons public accounts committee in 2014 showed that the royal household had been dipping into cash reserves to cover overspending, with the Queen's contingency fund falling from £35 million in 2001 to a historic low of £1 million.[37] The committee concluded that the royal household was 'not looking after nationally important heritage properties adequately', allowing too many of them to fall into disrepair; almost 40 per cent of the royal estate's buildings were not in an 'acceptable' condition in 2012. The committee heard that the state rooms at Buckingham Palace had not been redecorated or re-wired since 1952, while the boilers were sixty years old; asbestos needed to be removed from significant areas of the building; there were leaks in the roof of the picture gallery.[38] So much for the idea that the royals are fit and proper custodians of the country's heritage.

Opaque accounting, regular overspending and crumbling palaces: this is the real story about the state of the

---

37 *The Guardian*, 28 January 2014.

38 *Daily Mail*, 15 October 2013.

royal finances. There is no doubt that we could adopt a cheaper and more transparent option, with no loss of prestige. But the secrecy around royal finances needs to be seen in the context of an even larger problem, which is the extent to which the monarchy is allowed to withhold important information across the board. That's why we now need to look at the myth that they are 'above politics', a fiction colluded in not just by royal aides but by government ministers, historians and most of the press.

Natural-born Tories

There is an ignoble tradition here which stretches at least as far back as the 1930s. In those days a new king, Edward VIII, courted popularity with ordinary people by visiting impoverished communities but managed, for the most part, to conceal his support for the Nazi regime in Germany. This was, to be fair, an enthusiasm shared by the owners and editors of some British newspapers, most notably the *Daily Mail*; its proprietor, Lord Rothermere, wrote an article for his own paper in 1934 entitled 'Hurrah for the Blackshirts'. When Edward succeeded to the throne in 1936, diplomats at the German embassy in London cabled Hitler with an assurance that the new King urgently wanted an alliance between Britain and Germany.[39] Edward's reign was disastrous and thankfully short-lived, ending in his abdication after only eleven months so he could marry an American, Wallis Simpson; in 1937, shortly after their marriage, the couple ignored the advice of the British government and visited Germany. The new Duke and Duchess of Windsor met Hitler, had dinner with his deputy, Rudolf Hess, and visited a concentration camp. FBI documents released many years later appeared to suggest that Simpson's pro-Nazi views had alarmed the British Prime Minister, Stanley Baldwin, and it was those connections – not her status as a divorced woman – that meant that the King could not marry her and remain on the throne.[40] Despite all this, Edward VIII continues to be widely regarded as a misguided but

---

39 BBC News, profile of Edward VIII, 29 January 2003.

40 BBC News, 9 January 2003.

tragic figure who gave up the throne because he fell in love with a divorced woman. His brother, George VI, has recently been eulogised in a sentimental film, *The King's Speech*; the movie ends with the King overcoming his speech impediment in time to make a radio address to the nation after the government's declaration of war on Germany, a patriotic gesture which neatly erases his elder brother's dubious political sympathies.

In the twenty-first century, no one suspects members of the royal family of fascist sympathies, but the fact that they have partisan views is carefully spin-doctored out of public debate. In party terms, it is hard to believe that they are anything other than natural-born Tories, as an entry in the diaries of the former Labour MP Woodrow Wyatt, a close friend of the Queen Mother, appeared to confirm. In 1986, during a conversation with Wyatt about the following year, the Queen Mother suddenly asked whether it would 'be all right'; she was asking for an assurance, he explained, that Margaret Thatcher would win the next general election.[41]

---

41 *Daily Telegraph*, 31 March 2002.

Wyatt recorded that the Queen Mother 'adores Mrs Thatcher', an admiration apparently shared by other members of the family who often drank 'a toast at the end of dinner' to the Conservative Prime Minister. Another person the Queen Mother admired was P. W. Botha, the leader of apartheid-era South Africa who refused to release Nelson Mandela and was later found responsible for gross violations of human rights; she thought it was 'awful how the BBC and media misrepresent everything that Botha is trying to do'. She was less keen on the leaders of Commonwealth countries who argued for sanctions against South Africa, once describing President Kenneth Kaunda of Zambia as 'an idiot'. Wyatt also recorded that she liked Jews but thought they were a 'separate' and 'strange' people; he said she had 'some reservations about Jews in her old-fashioned English way'.[42] Such views would have been common among upper-middle-class women and indeed men of the Queen Mother's generation, where anti-Semitism and racism were never far

42 *The Guardian*, 19 July 2000.

below the surface. But they are hard to square with the unblemished reputation she enjoyed in her lifetime, casting her in the role of a wise and kindly matriarch. Nor is it easy to imagine her grandchildren or great-grandchildren voting Labour, even if they were eligible to do so.

Something happened in the autumn of 2014, however, that finally exploded the myth of an apolitical monarchy. Thanks to the Scottish referendum on independence, we now have an unequivocal example of the Queen intervening in politics at a moment of constitutional crisis. Naturally, she did it in such a way that it was left to the media to 'interpret' her remarks; given that the Queen's 'neutrality' is supposedly one of the strongest arguments for a constitutional monarchy, she is expert in letting her feelings be known without explicitly crossing the line into controversy. Here is what happened: just four days before the vote, when it was beginning to look as though the Scots might actually decide to break up the union, the Queen emerged from Crathie Kirk, the small parish church where members of the family worship when they are staying at Balmoral. Speaking to 'well-wishers' – that mysterious category of persons who only ever appear at royal events – she uttered these gnomic words to someone who asked about the imminent ballot: 'Well, I hope people will think very carefully about the future.'

Sensation! Hold the front page! The Queen and her advisers knew perfectly well how this apparently anodyne remark would be interpreted by the press, which duly reported it as a gesture of support for the 'no' camp. At the time, her intervention was widely reported as unexpected, although the context – a sudden surge in popularity for the 'yes' vote, suggesting that Scotland might choose independence – strongly suggests otherwise. Indeed, the fact that the whole thing was carefully staged was confirmed by the *Daily Telegraph*, which reported as follows:

> Although she usually walks between her car and the church without speaking to bystanders, she decided to do so after she left the church on the final Sunday before the referendum.
>
> Unusually, a police sergeant invited members of the press waiting 200 yards away to come up to the church

to see the royal party depart, *enabling them to hear her exchanges* [my italics].[43]

The same paper did the job it was supposed to do, spelling out what the Queen's words meant in a strapline: 'The monarch breaks her silence on Scottish independence four days before voters go to the polls, with her comments interpreted as support for a No vote.'

The *Daily Mail* went even further, describing the Queen's observation as a 'stark warning'[44] about independence.

What actually happened behind the scenes emerged three months later, when *The Guardian* laid out the high-level planning that went into her apparently off-the-cuff remark.[45] The paper reported that 'senior figures in Whitehall' were panicked by a YouGov poll published two weeks before the vote that showed a six-point drop in support for the 'no' campaign in the previous

---

43 *Daily Telegraph*, 14 September 2014.

44 *Daily Mail*, 14 September 2014.

45 *The Guardian*, 16 December 2014.

month; they approached Buckingham Palace, suggesting that an intervention from the Queen would be helpful. The situation became more critical during a subsequent visit to Balmoral by the Prime Minister, when the *Sunday Times* published the first opinion poll to show the 'yes' campaign ahead, if by the narrowest of margins (51 per cent). The shift in public opinion led to last-minute negotiations between the Cabinet Secretary, Sir Jeremy Heywood, and the Queen's private secretary, Sir Christopher Geidt; they came up with a 'carefully worded intervention' as No. 10 experienced what the paper described as a 'meltdown' over the prospect of a 'yes' vote. *The Guardian* then described precisely the process I outlined above:

> The two men are understood to have initially discussed the wisdom of a public intervention by the monarch, *who is scrupulously impartial*. Once it became clear that the Queen *was minded to speak out*, Geidt and Heywood then needed to fashion language which, while broadly neutral, *would leave nobody in any doubt about her support for the union* [my italics].

Even *The Guardian* cannot quite shake off the habit of claiming that the monarch does not intervene in politics, despite the fact that evidence to the contrary is staring it in the face. What the paper's scoop actually shows is this country's head of state engaging in an exercise to influence the way people vote, while maintaining a façade of 'neutrality'. Republic's CEO, Graham Smith, took the unusual step of calling on MPs to censure the Queen, saying she had overstepped the boundaries of her position:

> We would normally expect a head of state to take an active interest in such a momentous referendum, but the deal with the monarchy is that the monarch stays quiet and keeps out of these debates.
>
> The real problem is the system. But that doesn't excuse the Queen making her views known in such an underhand way while having her press office insist she is impartial.

Republic is right: this kind of behaviour is an affront to the democratic process, which rightly requires people who seek political outcomes to be open and transparent about their involvement. Anyone who genuinely supports democracy should be outraged by it.

And so they would be, were it not for the fact that the rise of a supposedly rambunctious press in the UK has made very little difference to the way the institution is scrutinised; the assumption that 'everybody' wants to know about the Queen and her relatives has spread through most of the media like mould in blue cheese, putting the royal soap opera on almost every front page. At the same time, the general public has very little knowledge of the royal family's extensive lobbying activities, carried out for the most part behind closed doors. While the public might be aware that Prince Charles dislikes modern architecture and is keen on 'alternative' medicine, most ordinary people continue to know little about how he uses his status to get privileged access to elected politicians; even fewer know that he and his mother have extraordinary powers of veto over proposed legislation. How many people are aware, for instance, that in 1999 the Queen vetoed a Private Member's Bill which would have transferred the power to authorise military strikes against Iraq from the monarch – herself, in other words

– to Parliament?[46] This species of interference is handled discreetly by royal aides and ministers' private secretaries, placing members of the family at one remove and shielding them from awkward questions about their political views. Hence the existence of the popular myth, which has great resonance at a time when elected politicians are held in low esteem, that the family floats above vulgar political disputes. I never believed this was true for a moment, given that people who enjoy power and influence are usually keen to make the most of it. My suspicions were confirmed when I attended a Christmas party at Buckingham Palace where I was introduced to the Queen – I think I can safely say she didn't take to me – and heard her talk about future membership of the EU in a way that clearly breached constitutional boundaries.

A Christmas turkey

The party was in a long gallery on the first floor of the palace, where some of the Queen's impressive art

---

46   Military Actions Against Iraq Bill, reported in *The Guardian*, 15 January 2013.

collection is crammed onto the walls. I was with my then partner Denis MacShane, who had been Europe minister at the Foreign Office until 2005 and was still a backbench MP. The first thing that struck me was how nervous and overawed most of the guests appeared to be at the prospect of being in the same room as the monarch. Isn't it a *sine qua non* that the head of state of a democratic country should make its citizens feel welcome and at ease? It is hard to see how that could happen at Buckingham Palace, where a suffocating atmosphere of protocol is reinforced by the presence of flunkies in antiquated court dress. One of the latter approached me and said that the Queen was about to arrive; was I prepared to be introduced to her? I said that I was and the courtier asked me and Denis to wait in a corner by the grand entrance doors. Several other couples joined us, including some Conservative MPs and their wives, and then the Queen walked into the room. She greeted Denis, whom she recognised, and he gestured towards me: 'May I introduce my partner, Joan Smith, who is a novelist.' I smiled and said 'hello'. The Queen looked aghast.

A silence spread between us; as well as failing to curtsy, I had broken the unspoken rule of not speaking until addressed by the monarch. Finally, as though I didn't exist, the Queen cut me dead and moved on to the Tory MP who was standing next to me. He introduced his wife, who curtsied, and the MP explained that she was Turkish. The Queen immediately looked brighter and said that she and her husband, Prince Philip, had been on a state visit to Turkey. The MP's wife nodded enthusiastically, saying how pleased people in Turkey had been about the visit. At this point, the Queen turned back to Denis. 'The EU is getting awfully big, twenty-eight countries,' she observed. Denis gently corrected her, pointing out that it was actually twenty-seven, and added: 'We're hoping Turkey will come in soon.' The Queen frowned. 'Oh no, we don't want Turkey to come in for a *long* time,' she said.

I simply do not believe that this is the only time, in her entire reign, that the Queen has uttered a controversial – and, indeed, unconstitutional – political opinion. If that were the case, how likely is it that this supposedly out-of-character event would be witnessed by a committed republican? It seems more likely to me that most people who meet the monarch are royalists, and they would not dream of repeating unguarded remarks which might damage her or the institution. When I mentioned the exchange on the BBC's *Newsnight* programme and published an account of it on my blog, it became a news story for the simple reason that it is so rare for anyone to tell the truth about such encounters. The Palace's response to a *Daily Telegraph* reporter was both awkward and sneakily *ad feminam*:

> Buckingham Palace declines to comment, but a courtier tells me: 'While it is not beyond the realms of possibility that Her Majesty made such a comment, it may have been taken out of context. The Queen has a good relationship with Turkey and Miss Smith is, I believe, a prominent republican.'[47]

The last line is a very good illustration of how the Palace operates, not directly accusing me of lying – there were too many witnesses to take that risk – but trying

---

47 *Daily Telegraph*, 23 April 2011.

to undermine me by mentioning my political views. At least I am open about them, unlike members of the royal family who habitually push pet causes behind the scenes.

The Queen sees the Prime Minister at weekly audiences but we know next to nothing about what is discussed on those occasions or about her meetings with other ministers; that would be acceptable in a system where the head of state had democratic legitimacy, but it is hard to justify when she is both unelected and unaccountable. A rare exception to this protective silence emerged when the BBC's security correspondent, Frank Gardner, revealed in a live interview on the *Today* programme that the Queen had told him she raised concerns with the government about the Egyptian cleric, Abu Hamza al-Masri. Abu Hamza, as he is usually known, was a deeply unpleasant Islamist who preached at the Finsbury Park mosque in north London; he fought a long and ultimately unsuccessful battle to avoid extradition to the US, where he faced trial on terrorism charges.[48] Gardner was talking about the case

---

48 BBC News, 25 September 2012.

in 2012, just after the European Court of Human Rights refused to refer Abu Hamza's case to the Grand Chamber, paving the way for his extradition. According to Gardner, the Queen told him she had raised the case with a former Home Secretary, asking why someone who incited hatred in his sermons had not been arrested earlier. 'Like anybody, she was upset that her country and its subjects were being denigrated by this man,' said Gardner.

There is no doubt that the cleric, who was accused of plotting to set up a terrorist camp in the US and involvement in abducting Western hostages in Yemen, was for a time the leading candidate for the title of 'most hated man in Britain'. But the Queen's intervention with the Cabinet minister responsible for the police, immigration and counter-terrorism was unwise to say the least; after the disclosure, which was unscripted, Gardner hurried on to say that this was not an instance of 'lobbying' and that the monarch was 'merely voicing the views that many have'. Of course 'many' people do not have privileged access to ministers, who would feel obliged to respond to anyone else that they could not (and should not) get involved in a case which was currently before the British or European courts. And while on this occasion the Queen's view was no doubt widely shared, that is unlikely to be the case every time she has direct access to a minister. What other subjects has she lobbied – sorry, voiced the views of many – on? We do not know, but the response to Gardner's revelation was in itself instructive. Within hours of the interview being broadcast, the story was no longer what the monarch said to a former Home Secretary but what the BBC's security correspondent had said to the presenter of the *Today* programme. In no time at all, the BBC was forced to make a grovelling apology to Buckingham Palace: 'The conversation should have remained private and the BBC and Frank deeply regret this breach of confidence. It was wholly inappropriate. Frank is extremely sorry for the embarrassment caused and has apologised to the Palace.'[49] The effect of such a stinging public rebuke to a senior broadcaster was, no doubt, to make other people think twice about revealing controversial remarks

---

49 BBC News, 25 September 2012.

by the Queen. Silence and the ability to maintain it is, as we have discovered, one of the monarchy's greatest protections.

We do know that Prince Charles is an assiduous networker, endlessly demanding private meetings with senior members of the government. In the three years following the 2010 general election, he held thirty-six private meetings with Cabinet ministers; the number of private audiences rises to fifty-three if meetings with junior ministers are included.[50] The election was held at the beginning of May and the Prince's first meeting with the Prime Minister, David Cameron, took place just two months later; they met once in 2011, three times in 2012, and twice in 2013. Charles was particularly keen to press his views on ministers at the Department for Environment, meeting three different ministers (including the then Secretary of State, Caroline Spelman) on five occasions. He was, if anything, even keener to get access to the top people at the Departments of Energy and Climate Change, meeting two secretaries of state

---

50 *Daily Mail*, 11 August 2013.

(Chris Huhne and Ed Davey) and two junior ministers over a series of seven meetings. In July 2013, Charles had an even more controversial meeting with the Health Secretary, Jeremy Hunt. The meeting came as critics complained that the NHS was wasting millions of pounds on homeopathy, an 'alternative' treatment dismissed by the government's chief scientific adviser, Sir Mark Walport, as 'nonsense'.[51] Charles was unhappy with these science-based verdicts on one of his pet therapies and went to the top, knowing that Hunt shares his views on 'alternative' therapies.

The Independent reported that several Labour MPs had reacted 'with fury' when they heard that Charles had lobbied Hunt, and not long afterwards they found support from an unexpected quarter. In a move which almost certainly reflects anxiety among monarchy-supporting newspapers about the prospect of Prince Charles ascending the throne, the *Daily Mail* joined the fray. It described his meetings with ministers as an 'extraordinary lobbying campaign' and suggested that

51 *The Independent*, 21 July 2013.

he was pushing favourite causes, including town planning and rural affairs. It described his views as 'strident' and even quoted a left-wing Labour MP, Paul Flynn, who accused the Prince of an 'incontinence of lobbying'. The paper said:

> The issue of Charles' opinions is becoming more and more relevant because he has recently started to take on more official duties from his 87-year-old mother…
>
> It is understood the majority of meetings were requested by the Prince rather than the ministers concerned. Minutes are not publicly available, with both sides refusing to disclose what is discussed.[52]

Charles is not always so reticent, making an unwise foray into international relations in 2014 when he compared the Russian President, Vladimir Putin, to Hitler. Many of us share his suspicions about the president of a country with a dreadful human rights record, but that is not the point: an unguarded remark of this kind, which

---

52 *Daily Mail*, 11 August 2013.

amounts to little more than an insult, was a headache for the British government and a gift to Putin. Shortly afterwards, the extent of the Prince's private lobbying became a little clearer when a number of Labour ex-ministers agreed to take part in a radio documentary.[53] A former Northern Ireland Secretary, Peter Hain, said that the Prince was delighted with the 'spectacularly good results' of a trial of complementary medicine in the province and tried to persuade the Welsh and White-hall governments to follow suit; neither department took any notice but Hain actually seems to have welcomed Charles's lobbying, as did a former Environment min-ister, Michael Meacher. He said he had worked with Charles to persuade Tony Blair to support green energy and block GM crops: 'We would consort together qui-etly in order to try and ensure that we increased our influence within government.' Meacher did at least acknowledge that the Prince was 'pushing it a bit' when he used his influence in this manner, but said he was delighted to have his support. Charles's interference

---

53 *The Royal Activist*, BBC Radio 4, 29 June 2014.

did not get such a welcome response from the former
Education Secretary, David Blunkett, who resisted the
Prince's lobbying to bring back grammar schools. 'I
would explain that our policy was not to expand grammar schools and he didn't like that,' Blunkett recalled.

'Black spider' memos

The democratic deficit implied by these lobbying activities is breathtaking. It is mainly thanks to *The Guardian*,
and in particular a reporter called Rob Evans, that they
have come under the spotlight at all; in a rare instance
of high-quality journalism about the monarchy, *The
Guardian* has spent *ten years* trying to force publication of a small selection of lobbying letters written
to ministers by the Prince. It is no secret that the heir
to the throne has reactionary and indeed anti-science
views; what the government doesn't want us to know
is *how* he lobbies on behalf of these causes, firing off
letter after letter which have become known (because
of his handwriting) as 'black spider' memos. Back in
2005, *The Guardian* made a modest FOI request to see

twenty-seven letters written in a seven-month period between 2004 and 2005. It was the beginning of an epic court battle which ended up at the Supreme Court in November 2014, where no fewer than six judges were asked to rule on the Attorney General's decision to over-rule a series of findings in favour of publication. At the time of writing, the Supreme Court's decision has not been announced, but this epic battle has already produced remarkable insights into Charles's autocratic behaviour.

Even before the matter reached the Supreme Court, the government had spent more than £250,000 in legal fees in a rearguard attempt to keep Charles's views secret, *and* threatened *The Guardian* with an application for full costs if its legal action was ultimately unsuccessful.[54] The reason ministers went to these lengths became apparent in September 2012, when an independent freedom of information tribunal ruled that the twenty-seven letters should be published. First of all, the tribunal dealt with the question of public interest, saying: 'The

---

54 *The Guardian*, 28 March 2014.

essential reason is that it will generally be in the overall public interest for there to be transparency as to how and when Prince Charles seeks to influence government.'[55]

It went on to argue that lobbying by the heir to the throne 'cannot have constitutional status' and should not be protected from disclosure. Crucially, its members said that the evidence revealed:

> Prince Charles using his access to government ministers, and no doubt considering himself entitled to use that access, in order to set up and drive forward charities and promote views, *but not as part of his preparation for kingship* ... Ministers responded, and no doubt felt themselves obliged to respond, *but again not as part of Prince Charles's preparation for kingship* [my italics].

What the letters reveal, in other words, is Prince Charles using his position and status to force ministers to respond to his views, even though he has no constitutional right to do so. In normal politics, where

---

55 *The Guardian*, 16 October 2012.

transparency is quite properly an issue, this kind of covert influence-seeking would be seen as improper, if not calling into question someone's suitability to hold public office. The then Attorney General, Dominic Grieve, moved swiftly to protect the Prince, announcing that he was vetoing publication. Two years later, at the Court of Appeal, three judges ruled that Grieve had acted unlawfully. They said he did not have reasonable grounds to veto publication and ordered him to pay *The Guardian*'s costs, which by then amounted to £96,000. Grieve is a decent man who won a Lifetime Achievement Award from the human rights campaign group Liberty after his sacking from government in 2014, so it was sad to see him pursuing this battle against transparency with such vigour.

Fortunately for those of us who believe in accountability, Grieve's explanation of why he went to such lengths to keep the content of the letters secret had already given the game away. Grieve frankly admitted that he used the veto because the public could interpret the letters as 'disagreeing with government policy'. It is a cornerstone of the British constitution that the monarch cannot be seen to favour one political party over another; hence any perception that Charles disagreed with a Labour government 'would be seriously damaging to his role as future monarch because, if he forfeits his position of political neutrality as heir to the throne, he cannot easily recover it when he is king'.[56]

I don't believe this is about perception: it is about a senior member of the royal family challenging the policies of an elected government. That alone makes him unfit to succeed his mother as head of state, when ministers will no doubt find his lobbying even harder to resist. Don't forget that this case is about only a tiny batch of the hundreds of letters Charles fires off, which Grieve described as 'in many cases particularly frank' and reflecting the Prince's 'most deeply held personal views and beliefs'. They were addressed to ministers at a wide range of departments, including Business, Innovation and Skills; Health; Children, Schools and Families; Environment, Food and Rural Affairs; Culture, Media and Sport; the Northern Ireland Office and the Cabinet

---

56　*The Guardian*, 12 March 2014.

Office.[57] We also have some idea, from the information tribunal's ruling, of the subjects he raised: 'holistic' medicine, genetically modified crops, cuts in the armed forces, architecture and agricultural policy.[58] It does not take much ingenuity to guess his views on any of these subjects, which are doubtless typical of a socially conservative landowner with a prejudice against allopathic medicine. In a telling paragraph in their 126-page ruling, the three judges conceded that Charles's activities 'are not neutral and in a number of respects have been controversial'. The government has now imposed a blanket ban so that even if this batch of the Prince's letters is finally forced into the open, later ones will remain secret.

But covert lobbying is by no means the only way in which the Prince gets his way on matters of public policy and indeed legislation. He also has special powers in his role as Duke of Cornwall, a title which makes him beneficiary of a private landholding which provides an annual income of just over £17 million. His consent is

---

57 *Evening Standard*, 13 March 2014.

58 *The Guardian*, 18 September 2012.

required for legislation which affects the 'hereditary revenues, personal property or other interests'[59] of the Duchy, and in recent years he has been invited to give his consent to new legislation on everything from the London Olympics to shipwrecks. Documents released in 2012 show that the Labour government's fisheries minister, Huw Irranca-Davies, wrote to the Prince's private secretary in 2008 enclosing two copies of a draft marine and coastal access bill. He highlighted clauses which would require the Prince's consent and got a response a couple of months later, informing him that 'the Prince of Wales is content with the bill'.[60] This archaic formula is bad enough – I am not 'content' with many pieces of legislation, such as the bedroom tax, but I quite rightly don't have a veto over them – yet Prince Charles is not the only member of the family to benefit from these far-reaching powers. I've already mentioned the occasion in 1999 when the Queen vetoed a Private Member's Bill, a fact which emerged as a consequence of another FOI

---

59 *The Guardian*, 30 October 2011.

60 *The Guardian*, 18 September 2012.

request. Tellingly, the request, which revealed a treasure trove of material about royal interference, was not made by a journalist; it came from a legal scholar named John Kirkhope, who wanted to see papers relating to the royal veto for use in his graduate studies at the University of Plymouth. The government fought to keep the papers secret for fifteen months, and it isn't difficult to see why.

After ministers lost the case, the Cabinet Office was forced to release an internal Whitehall pamphlet which revealed that at least thirty-nine bills had been affected by powers allowing members of the royal family to veto or consent to proposed legislation.[61] The Queen and Prince Charles had been asked to approve bills on subjects as varied as higher education, paternity pay, ID cards, civil partnerships and even high hedges. Civil servants were warned that 'a major plank' of bills would have to be removed if either the Queen or the Prince withheld consent; even when consent was granted, any amendments to bills would also have

---

61 *The Guardian*, 15 January 2013.

to be submitted for royal approval, a process which could delay progress of the legislation through Parliament. According to *The Guardian*: 'Charles has been asked to consent to twenty pieces of legislation and this power of veto has been described by constitutional lawyers as a royal "nuclear deterrent" that may help explain why ministers appear to pay close attention to the views of senior royals.'[62]

The royals' supposed lack of power and influence is the most pernicious of all public fantasies, worse even than the sentimental outpourings that accompany the family's engagements, marriages and births. It allows the Queen and her relatives to retain a species of unaccountability denied, rightly, to all institutions which receive public funding – and many that don't. We expect MPs, government ministers, the police, the legal profession, doctors, even the press, to be open about what they are doing and acknowledge mistakes. The British monarchy is an exception to this principle and many others, a relic from periods of history when all that mattered

---

62 Ibid.

was getting and retaining power. It is a system of government which has been tried and rejected all over the world, as we shall see in the next section.

Part III

Up with democracy

I T I S S O M E T I M E S easy to forget, looking at monarchy from a purely British perspective, what a strange creature it is. The reality is that it's on its way out, leaving only around twenty-five families in the entire world who enjoy these unique privileges by an accident of birth. Fewer than a quarter (forty-three) of the world's nations are monarchies, and even that figure is inflated by the fact that Elizabeth II is monarch of sixteen Commonwealth nations. It is worth mentioning here that she is also Head of the Commonwealth, an organisation with a combined population of 2.1 billion people, yet her role is neither elected nor subject to a fixed term. The Commonwealth's governance includes a vague statement that the choice of the next head 'will be made collectively by Commonwealth leaders' but no mechanism is set out; the widespread expectation is that Prince Charles will seamlessly succeed his mother.

None of the world's largest democracies – India, Indonesia or the US – has a hereditary head of state or displays any enthusiasm for having one. When India became independent in 1947, many of its maharajas agreed to sign over their ancestral territory and palaces to the new state; in 1972, the Prime Minister, Indira Gandhi, stripped them of their remaining titles and privileges. Even when quasi-royal dynasties arise and dominate the political scene, as the Nehrus/Gandhis did for a time in India, the democratic process asserts itself in the end.

The list of countries that ceased to be monarchies in the twentieth century is too long to rehearse in its entirety but it includes Italy, Egypt, Tunisia, China, Germany, Yugoslavia, Turkey, Greece, Albania, Romania, Iraq, Libya, Vietnam, Portugal, Russia, Syria, Iceland and Mongolia. Kings, emirs, kaisers, queens, maharajas, grand-dukes, princes and czars found themselves out on their ears, sometimes in farcical circumstances; in 1952,

Egypt's last monarch, the playboy King Farouk, was allowed to leave the country on the royal yacht as long as he promised to send it back when he arrived in exile in Italy. On paper, Farouk had abdicated in favour of his infant son, who became Fuad II, but the country was declared a republic the following year; Farouk continued to pursue a lavish lifestyle, swelling to almost 300 lbs in weight and dying of a heart attack, aged forty-five, in 1963. Russia's last czar, Nicholas II, was even less fortunate, dying with his family in Yekaterinburg, a town in the Urals, when the revolutionary government ordered his murder in 1918. Nicholas was a relative of George V and looked uncannily like him, but the King refused his cousin's desperate plea for asylum in the UK after his abdication at the time of the revolution a year earlier. Family feeling counts for less than one might think among the royals, but the gruesome fate of the Romanovs has since been transformed into a romantic myth, celebrated in films like *Nicholas and Alexandra*.

In Europe, around a dozen of Europe's fifty countries retain some form of monarchical system, although three of them – Liechtenstein, Luxembourg and Monaco

– are almost too small to count. The Monégasque royal family has a public presence out of all proportion to the size of the principality, chiefly because the late Prince Rainier III made the astute move of marrying an American film star, Grace Kelly. Their children have a permanent presence in gossip magazines, where their marriages, divorces and indeed paternity suits provide reams of copy. The current incumbent, Prince Albert II, has two 'illegitimate' children and spent years refusing to acknowledge paternity; DNA tests in 2005 and 2006 established beyond doubt that he was the father of both children but they remain excluded by law from the royal succession. The Grimaldis are typical royal hedonists, in other words, enjoying an existence similar to that of the pop stars, soap stars and models who populate the pages of *Hello!* magazine. This is true of many of the world's remaining monarchies, although some do a better job than others of concealing their excesses from the people they rule; in 2005, the town of Marbella in Andalusia declared three days of mourning for King Fahd of Saudi Arabia, who liked to spend his summers there rather than at home in his strictly

religious kingdom, where alcohol and gambling are for-
bidden. Fahd's visits to Marbella began in the 1970s and
he eventually owned a 200-acre estate outside the town
equipped with a private clinic, a mosque, several palaces
and a sports complex. After his death, *The Guardian*
listed his entourage with something approaching awe:

> On his last visit, the king arrived with a fleet of jumbo jets
> and about 3,000 family members, friends, camp followers
> and staff. He booked 300 hotel rooms, hired 500 additional
> staff, and more than 100 new Mercedes cars arrived on
> transporters from Germany, where they had been leased.[63]

Europe's monarchies do not have wealth on this scale
but they are self-indulgent in their tastes, even after the
2008 financial crisis. It accounts, among other things, for
the dramatic collapse in support for Spain's monarchy
in recent years. Juan Carlos I was hailed as a bulwark
of democracy in 1975 when he assumed the throne after
the death of the dictator General Franco, putting an end

---

63 *The Guardian*, 6 August 2005.

to one of Europe's most enduring tyrannies. Few people would have imagined, at the time, that his subsequent loss of public esteem would be so precipitous as to force his abdication almost four decades later. In 2014, Juan Carlos stepped down in favour of his son, whose accession as Felipe VI prompted republican demonstrations in many Spanish cities. Like Prince Albert of Monaco, Juan Carlos had been dogged by rumours of affairs and embarrassing paternity suits; shortly after he gave up the throne, the Spanish Parliament tried to cut off further scandals by passing a law to give him immunity from such actions.[64] But these were far from being the only gaffes which humiliated his Queen and turned people against him; the most egregious was a free trip to Botswana in 2012 where Juan Carlos, who was then honorary President of the Spanish branch of the World Wildlife Fund, went on safari to shoot elephants. The trip came to light only because the elderly King fell, broke his hip and had to be airlifted back to a Spanish hospital.[65] Then there was

---

64 *The Guardian*, 26 June 2014.

65 *The Guardian*, 4 March 2013.

the scandal around his son-in-law, Iñaki Urdangarin, a former Olympic athlete who married the King's younger daughter, the Infanta Cristina. In June 2014, less than a week after her brother ascended the Spanish throne, a court upheld corruption charges against the Princess in a case involving Urdangarin, who was accused of fraud, falsifying documents and embezzlement.[66] Five months later, Cristina failed in an attempt to have the charges dropped; at the time of writing, the couple are awaiting trial. An opinion poll published less than a week after the King's abdication suggested that the gesture was not enough; two-thirds of the Spanish population demanded a referendum on the future of the monarchy, a choice they have so far been denied.[67]

Keeping up the illusion

The Spanish experience is a warning to royalists that support for monarchy can evaporate virtually overnight,

66 *The Guardian*, 25 June 2014.

67 *The Guardian*, 8 June 2014.

especially in difficult financial times such as those that followed the 2008 financial crisis. The *Washington Post*, reflecting on the Spanish abdication, posed what might have seemed an unthinkable question even two decades earlier, asking whether Europe's remaining monarchies – 'mostly fusty, toothless institutions' – should go.[68] This verdict from the other side of the Atlantic underestimates their remaining power and influence, as we have already seen. But it is a reminder of how archaic Europe's monarchies seem to nations which have been republics for decades and in some cases centuries.

In the UK, where a sophisticated PR effort goes into normalising the continued existence of a royal dynasty, this is not so apparent; on the contrary, one of the curious side effects of the Windsors' longevity has been to turn London into a favoured hang-out for deposed monarchs, many of them related to the British royal family. The Duke of Edinburgh's cousin, King Constantine II of Greece, ended up in Hampstead after being overthrown in a right-wing coup in 1967; six years later, the

---

68 *Washington Post*, 2 June 2014.

junta declared Greece a presidential republic, a decision
endorsed in a referendum when democratic government
returned the following year. But some people never give
up: 'King Constantine and Queen Anne-Marie of the
Hellenes' appeared on the guest list for Prince William's
wedding in 2011; so, by the way, did a couple called
'Crown Prince Alexander and Crown Princess Kath-
erine of Yugoslavia', a country which was torn apart by
civil war in the 1990s and no longer exists.[69] Another
royal dynasty, the Pahlavis, set up camp in a hotel in
Kensington after the Shah of Iran was overthrown in
a coup in 1979; they lived within walking distance of
Kensington Palace, where the divorced Princess Diana
– also experiencing a species of exile – would one day
plot and seethe against her former in-laws.

The violent overthrow of so many royal dynasties is
a potent argument for the democratic process, which
offers a peaceful and dignified exit for people whose
privileges are long past their sell-by date. The map of
Europe might look very different if they accepted this

---

69 *The Guardian*, 26 April 2011.

option: European monarchies have not fared well on the rare occasions when ordinary people have actually been allowed a vote on the matter; the Italian monarchy was ended by a referendum in 1946, long before the Greeks confirmed their desire to be a republic. On the other side of the world, Australia is usually cited as an example of the popularity of the British royal family, following the 55 per cent vote in 1999 in favour of keeping the Queen as head of state. But that referendum can hardly be counted as a true test of republican sentiment, given that it failed to offer a democratic alternative; the option on offer was not a republic with an elected head of state but the unpopular alternative of a President appointed by Parliament.

From a modern perspective, it is clear that monarchy is a pre-modern form of government. The constitutional model adopted by the UK supposedly addresses some of the criticisms, yet the Windsors have steadfastly resisted even the modest reforms associated with the Dutch and Scandinavian royal families – the so-called 'bicycling' monarchies. Even in those countries, the changes have been cosmetic, a matter of personal style rather than constitutional significance, but the notion of the Queen (even in her younger days) or Princes Charles getting on their bikes is unthinkable. The result is a bewildering gap between the UK's commitment to modernity, expressed in domestic law and international treaties, and a constitutional arrangement which gives so much status and influence to a single family. The UK was one of the countries that drew up the UN Declaration of Human Rights, which was adopted by the UN general assembly almost six decades ago and is still widely regarded as the pre-eminent statement of the rights of human beings. The very first article declares that 'all human beings are born equal in dignity and rights', a proposition which is simply impossible to square with the institution of monarchy.

Daring to be modern

It takes a bit of imagination to get beyond the idea of the UK as a top-down society with the same family always at the summit. An Asian friend once told me that there are villages in India where girls who haven't been able to find husbands are married to a tree; it is better to be married to a non-human object, so the argument runs, than not to be married at all. There is an analogy here: the British royal family is *our* tree, something people lean on because they haven't given any thought to what life might be like without it. The answer is less scary than they might think; I'm tempted to adapt the old feminist slogan and suggest that a modern democracy needs a queen like a fish needs a bicycle. The benefits of becoming a republic far outweigh any nostalgic attachment to the late Princess Diana or rose-tinted memories of royal weddings.

So how would an elected President differ from the current arrangement? The first thing to go would be the hideous *cronyism* that is such a blot on the record of the British royal family. It is highly unlikely that a head of state, elected by popular vote and with the option of standing for a second term, would keep the kind of unsavoury company favoured by the Windsors. As well as a fair number of deluded ex-monarchs, vainly dreaming of being welcomed home by cheering crowds, the guest list for the 2011 royal wedding was notable for the number of indefensible regimes that were represented. One of them was Lesotho, a small country in south-east Africa which has been accused of a catalogue of human rights abuses: torture, deaths in police custody, corruption, trafficking, discrimination against people with HIV/Aids, and child labour.[70] But the invitation that caused most outrage was to the Gulf state of Bahrain, whose Crown Prince Salman bin Hamad bin Isa al-Khalifa was on the list, even while his father the King remained at home suppressing an uprising with brutal force. 'How does the Queen justify her invitation to an unelected tyrant with fresh blood on his hands?' the *New Statesman* demanded.[71]

On the day before the wedding, I joined the human rights activist Peter Tatchell for a demonstration at the gates of Buckingham Palace, where we unfurled a banner protesting about Prince Salman's inclusion on the guest list. Supporters of the monarchy squirmed and claimed that the royal family had no choice but to invite heads

---

70 US State Department, Lesotho Human Rights Report.

71 *New Statesman*, 17 March 2011.

of state, but the excuse was blasted out of the water by the Foreign Office: a spokesman categorically denied that the wedding was a state occasion, arguing that it was 'a private wedding so invitations are down to Clarence House'.[72] Faced with a torrent of bad publicity so close to the wedding, Prince Salman made a last-minute announcement that he would not attend. King Abdullah of Saudi Arabia, who had recently sent troops to support the Khalifa family's crackdown in Bahrain, had no such qualms, sending Prince Mohammed bin Nawaf bin Abdul Aziz to represent him. But then members of the Saudi royal family are known to be particular friends of the groom's father, Prince Charles.

This episode is a reminder that the Windsors associate with tyrants *by choice*, a fact demonstrated by how often Charles visits absolute monarchies with terrible human rights records; he doesn't even seem to mind that the Saudis bear a heavy responsibility for exporting Wahabbism, a particularly unpleasant form of Islam which imposes barbaric punishments under sharia law.

---

72 *The Week*, 17 March 2011.

The cost of these jaunts to taxpayers is stupendous: in 2011, a visit by Prince Charles and Camilla to the Middle East and Africa cost £460,387 after they chartered a private plane for the entire trip.[73] Nothing is too undignified for the UK's future head of state: in February 2014, Charles took part in a ceremony in a stadium in Riyadh hosted by the former head of Saudi intelligence, Prince Muqrin bin Abdulaziz, where he joined in a sword dance.[74] In Saudi Arabia, swords are generally used for a more sinister purpose: a few months after Charles's visit, Amnesty International documented twenty-three executions, most of them beheadings, in just three weeks; they included two sets of brothers on 18 August, all of whom claimed to have been tortured during interrogation.[75] On the same trip, Charles visited Qatar, which has been described together with the Saudi kingdom as 'major culprits in the exploitation

---

73 *Daily Telegraph*, 2 July 2012.

74 *The Guardian*, 19 February 2014.

75 Saudi Arabia: Scheduled beheading reflects authorities' callous disregard to human rights, Amnesty International, 22 August 2014.

and ill-treatment of migrant workers', who are often subjected to financial exploitation, beatings, torture, rape and execution.[76] No matter: Charles's connections with the Emir of Qatar came in useful when he took a dislike to a £3 billion scheme by a London-based architect, Christian Candy, working with a Qatari company to redevelop the Chelsea Barracks site in London. The scheme was dropped at the last minute and Candy sued the Qatari company in the High Court, where it was alleged that Charles had lobbied the royal family to get the scheme withdrawn.[77] A letter Charles sent to the Qatari Prime Minister in March 2009 was revealed in court, showing the Prince complaining about 'brutalist' architecture in the city and pushing the merits of an alternative neo-classical scheme by his favourite architect, Quinlan Terry.[78] Two months later, Charles met the Emir for tea at Clarence House and the court heard that

---

76 Migrant workers in Qatar and Saudi Arabia suffer extreme abuse and human rights violations, Children's Human Rights Network, Amnesty International, 24 December 2013.

77 *Daily Mail*, 16 May 2010.

78 Building.co.uk., 25 June 2010.

the ruler subsequently 'went mental' with the head of the Qatari company, echoing Charles's view of 'how awful the scheme was'.[79] Not only did Candy win his case, but the judge condemned Charles's intervention as 'unexpected and unwelcome'. The Royal Institute of British Architects, whose members have suffered interference from Charles on many occasions, said that the case highlighted 'inappropriate behind-the-scenes methods used by the Prince of Wales' to stop the Chelsea Barracks scheme.[80] Its architect, Lord Rogers, later claimed that the Prince effectively has a veto over planning applications in London, accusing him of 'unconstitutional behaviour' and an 'abuse of power'.[81]

It is not just the Queen's eldest son who enjoys connections with unsavoury regimes. His younger brother, the Duke of York, is such an avid traveller that he has earned the nickname 'Air Miles Andy'. As well as the usual clutch of princes from Gulf states, he is on friendly

---

79 *Financial Times*, 25 June 2010.

80 RIBA response to Chelsea Barracks judgment.

81 *Evening Standard*, 23 August 2013.

terms with politicians and oligarchs from Azerbaijan, Turkmenistan and Kazakhstan, former Soviet republics with poor human rights records. During the Prince's ten-year stint as a UK trade envoy, most of his trips were paid for by taxpayers, with the cost amounting to £358,763 in 2010 alone;[82] he stepped down from the role in the middle of the following year, but his publicly funded travel bill *rose* by £20,000, including £81,000 for a single trip via a chartered flight to Saudi Arabia.[83] (The Prince once chartered an aircraft for a two-day trip to Teesside and Belfast, at a cost of £10,470.) This is despite the fact that Andrew's role as trade envoy was marred by a series of bad decisions, usually involving close relatives of despotic leaders; early in 2011, the Labour MP Chris Bryant called for the Prince to be sacked from his job promoting trade, claiming in Parliament that he was a 'very close friend' of Colonel Gaddafi's second son, Saif al-Islam, who was later charged with two counts of crimes against humanity by the International Criminal

---

82 *Daily Mail*, 26 November 2011.

83 *Daily Telegraph*, 2 July 2012.

Court.[84] Andrew also held a lunch at Buckingham Palace for Sakher el-Materi, son-in-law of the Tunisian dictator Zine el Abidine Ben Ali, just three months before the regime was overthrown in the revolution that kicked off the Arab Spring in 2011;[85] some people, it seems, just can't help being on the wrong side of history.

But the connection that cast greatest doubt on Andrew's judgement – and finally caused him to stand down as trade envoy – was his friendship with the American multi-millionaire and convicted sex offender Jeffrey Epstein. The financier owned a mansion in Palm Beach, Florida, and in 2005 a woman complained to police that he had assaulted her fourteen-year-old daughter at his home. The FBI began an investigation and up to forty young women, some of them aged between fourteen and sixteen at the time, claimed they had been procured for sex at the mansion. In 2008, Epstein entered a plea bargain, pleading guilty to soliciting prostitution with an

---

84 Situation in Libya: The Prosecutor v Said Al-Islam Gaddafi, Case No. ICC-01/11-01/11, International Criminal Court, warrant of arrest issued 27 June 2011.

85 *The Guardian*, 4 March 2011.

under-age girl; he was sentenced to eighteen months in prison and served thirteen months. On Epstein's release, Andrew continued to see him and he was even photographed walking with the financier – now a registered sex offender – in New York's Central Park. Newspaper reports suggest that the Prince eventually broke the connection but the damage was done, landing the British royal family with the worst set of headlines it has endured in decades: 'Andrew denies sex slave claims: Prince is named in US lawsuit' (*Daily Express*) and 'I was Andy's sex slave: Palace's fury at shock court claims in States' (*The Sun*). The accusations emerged in early January 2015 after a woman filed a motion in a Florida court claiming that Epstein had 'loaned' her for sex with wealthy and well-connected friends, including Prince Andrew, when she was seventeen (and thus a minor under Florida law). Buckingham Palace initially refused to comment but later changed its mind and issued no fewer than four categorical denials of 'any suggestion of impropriety with under-age minors' on the Prince's part.[86]

---

86 BBC News, 4 January 2015.

An elected head of state who behaved like the Queen's two elder sons, using public funds on a profligate scale to visit regimes accused of flagrant human rights abuses, would risk being ejected by voters at the next election; someone who covertly used his or her connections to destroy a commercial deal might even end up being impeached. That is how the democratic process works, maintaining checks and balances so that no individual becomes too powerful. But the Windsors are immovable under present constitutional arrangements and their position at the top of the social structure plays a key role in maintaining the UK's class system. This is another unappealing feature of 'modern' Britain which would look very different under a republic, reducing at a stroke the huge number of people directly employed by or dependent on the royal family for patronage of one sort or another; royalty institutionalises deference, the notion that some people deserve respect solely on account of who they are – their birthright, in other words – and hence *condescension* and *snobbery* are built into the system. There are few better places to see this in action than a Buckingham Palace garden party, when thousands of people from all over the country are invited to drink tea on the palace lawn and mingle, at a safe distance, with the royals. There isn't even a pretence of equality as the masses are guided towards a huge marquee, kept well away from the more favoured guests who make for the smaller and more exclusive diplomatic and royal tents. One July afternoon, when the event was wrecked by a sudden downpour of monsoon proportions, I heard an announcement that the royal family was being 'evacuated' into the palace, while the rest of us were left to huddle, as best we could, in the inadequate shelter of the big marquee. Few complained, because the key to this system is everyone knowing their place and being thankful for the tiny advantages – in this case, being in the palace garden at all – that come with it.

The popularity of TV dramas such as *Upstairs, Downstairs* and *Downton Abbey* is often attributed to nostalgia, suggesting that viewers enjoy watching a social hierarchy that now seems quaint and outmoded. But the army of volunteers who show visitors around National Trust properties confirms the persistence of an opposing and profoundly undemocratic narrative;

uncritically affirming the social status of previous owners, they send a message that birth and wealth matter as
much as they ever did in the UK. This is a paradox in a
country where millions of voters regularly turn out to
support parties whose manifestos claim a commitment
to equality and social justice – though not, as we have
seen, an elected head of state – and so is the fact that
the Queen enjoys immense powers of *nepotism*. She
exercises these first and foremost to the benefit of her
immediate relatives, showering them with titles in lieu of
(or in addition to) the usual birthday and wedding gifts.
In 1987, she decided that Princess Anne would in future
be known as the Princess Royal, a title restricted to the
monarch's eldest daughter; in 2011, she celebrated her
grandson William's wedding by conferring the title of
Duke and Duchess of Cambridge on him and his bride.
(The couple even have a spare title, Earl and Countess
of Strathearn, for use when they cross the border into
Scotland.) Prince Andrew got a royal dukedom when
he married Sarah Ferguson, although the Duchess of
York has complained of being frozen out of the family
since her divorce. The Dukedom of Windsor is vacant

and seems likely to remain so, given its unfortunate history, but the Queen has plenty of other baubles to dangle down the chain. Honours come in minute gradations, bewildering to foreigners but clearly understood by those who hope to receive them; a CBE is worth more than an OBE, for instance, and that in turn is better than an MBE. So significant are these distinctions that I once heard about a former British ambassador who was distraught to receive a common-or-garden knighthood when he had expected a KCMG; both entitle the holder to be addressed as 'Sir' but a 'Knight Commander of the Order of St Michael and St George' (satirically known as 'Kindly Call Me God') is much posher.

I was more than a little surprised, in view of my republicanism, to receive a letter in 2003 offering me an MBE for 'services to human rights'. I didn't think about accepting it for a moment because the Order of the British Empire is so closely associated with the royal family; dished out by the Queen and Prince Charles at twice-yearly investitures, its motto is 'For God and the Empire'. It is outrageous that a citizen of a 21st-century democracy can be honoured by the state only if he or she buys into this edifice of royal flummery. I'm not against the state recognising outstanding achievement, but it could just as easily be done through a secular and egalitarian Order of Britain. The reaction to my refusal was revealing in itself, showing how widely the snobbery of the honours system has taken hold in unexpected quarters, including journalism: one friend told me I'd done the right thing because he thought I deserved 'more' than an MBE; another wrote an angry newspaper column, implying that if I didn't want it, he wouldn't mind having it in my place. There *is* an option of accepting an honour without receiving it in person, but it's clearly frowned upon; a well-known writer who turned down a trip to Buckingham Palace told me he was later left off the list when the country's foremost novelists were invited to a reception by the Queen.

Along with the monarchy, it's time for the whole rigmarole of royal dukes, hereditary peers, earls and knights to be consigned to history. (It actually made no sense to expel unelected hereditary peers from the House of Lords, where they were able to pass legislation, while retaining the far greater privileges of the unelected royal family.) That would allow the UK to become the egalitarian nation it already claims to be; for the growing numbers of people who are getting involved in Republic's campaign for an elected head of state, the idea of the UK as a species of royal theme park is long past its sell-by date. Just about every recent political development is moving in the same direction, whether it is the demand for greater devolution in Scotland and England or legal powers for constituents to recall MPs. Indeed, it is ironic that most of the accusations hurled at MPs, reasonably or otherwise, since the expenses scandal of 2009 apply with even greater force to the royal family: distance from ordinary people, lack of accountability, absence of transparency, profligacy with public money. But while MPs who behave badly are subject to parliamentary scrutiny and can be ejected from office at the next election, nothing in our political system can protect us from the accession of a monarch who has already shown himself unfit to represent the country.

Anxiety about the heir apparent emerges in unexpected places, as this headline from the *Daily Mail* reveals: 'Why Prince Charles is too dangerous to be king:

in a landmark essay Max Hastings tells why this increasingly eccentric royal could imperil the monarchy'.[87] Even without anything approaching a genuine debate, it is clear that a substantial number of people – around a quarter of the population – do not want Prince Charles to succeed his mother. According to a YouGov media briefing in the wake of the diamond jubilee, 'Our polls are consistent in showing a significant minority of people who think Charles will not do well in the role of King.'[88] Although Charles has since recovered some ground, a poll at this time showed that 44 per cent would prefer the throne to pass directly to William. Clearly, despite this country having been a monarchy for centuries, a significant number of people do not understand the principle of primogeniture; in a constitutional monarchy, it is of no consequence if the heir to the throne is a dud. Charles III, or whatever he decides to call himself when he ascends the throne, will be the next head of state whether we like it or not. Nor does he intend to

---

87 Mail Online, 18 December 2010.

88 YouGov: Recent YouGov polling on the Monarchy and the Jubilee.

change his ways: 'friends' of the Prince told *The Guardian* that he will go on making 'heartfelt interventions' on subjects he feels passionately about when he becomes King.[89] It is a curious fact that people seem less concerned about this eventuality than they are about the bogeyman of 'President Blair', a prospect from which we are protected by the most significant feature of any democratic system. Anyone who wanted to become our elected President would have to win the popular vote, and it is hard to imagine a politician more widely disliked or distrusted than the former Prime Minister.

In the end, trust is at the heart of this matter. It is a paradox that we trust ourselves to elect MPs and hence the government of the day, made up of individuals with the power to make laws, set tax rates and even take us to war against other countries, yet we don't trust ourselves to choose the person who carries out an equally important but ceremonial job, representing our values on the public stage and pulling us together at moments of crisis. No matter how much the country changes,

---

89 *The Guardian*, 20 November 2014.

we are always represented by the same mono-cultural individuals who look nothing like so many of us. Why should one section of the population – white, conservative, upper middle class, publicly heterosexual, Christian – have a monopoly on how the nation presents itself to the world? Why can't I and people like me have an opportunity to vote for someone whose values are closer to ours? I can think of many individuals who would do the job with greater warmth and spontaneity than the Queen or Prince Charles – the author Philip Pullman, the human rights campaigner Pragna Patel or the artist Grayson Perry, for instance. In a world dominated by celebrity, it would be refreshing if less well-known people decided to stand, using social networking sites to launch their campaigns. I wouldn't even mind if a member of the former royal family put him or herself forward as candidate, although I wouldn't vote for them. No matter who was elected, we could choose someone else next time if they didn't do a good job.

What I do mind is the fact that the same bland and unrepresentative woman has been head of state longer than I've been alive. I'm embarrassed when British politicians and athletes are expected to mumble 'God Save the Queen' at public events, demonstrating an affection some of them don't actually feel, as well as the fact that very few of us know more than the first verse. I have no doubt that a country as diverse and culturally rich as ours, with such a huge range of talent in business, politics, medicine, law and the arts, can do better than this. If anything, the question of what we look like to the world has been made more urgent by the Scottish referendum; I don't want to live in an increasingly disunited kingdom, torn apart by competing forms of nationalism. A republic of England, Scotland, Wales and Northern Ireland is long overdue, and so is the opportunity to celebrate the values – equality, fairness and compassion – that bind us together. In the twenty-first century, we shouldn't still be imploring an imaginary deity to save an inherited head of state. If we can only find the courage, we are perfectly capable of saving ourselves.

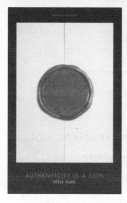